Ohio's Lake Erie Islands
A Brief History in Words and Pictures

"Our days have passsed too swiftly by! We have found this beautiful
island home constantly reminding us that this world is not our abiding
place — for we have yearned to remain here forever — it cannot be..."
Jay Cooke, June 1865

Ohio's Lake Erie Islands

A Brief History in Words and Pictures

Words and Photography by
Chad Waffen

Westfalia Publishing Group
Bay Village, Ohio

Ohio's Lake Erie Islands

A Brief History in Words and Pictures

Published by:

W **Westfalia Publishing Group**
Bay Village, Ohio
westfaliapublishing@netlink.net

Second Edition

Text and Photography © 2010, 2006 by Chad Waffen, Westfalia Publishing

West Sister Island image courtesy John Marvin,

Marvin Aerial Photography, www.greatlakeslighthouses.com

ISBN 0-9777891-0-1

Library of Congress Control Number 2006921667

SAN 850-2439

Printed in China

Cover: Sunrise on Kelleys Island   Previous pages: Sunset on Kelleys Island

Dedicated to David R. Wolf,
whose contagious enthusiasm for the island lifestyle
was an inspiration to anyone who had the opportunity
to visit him on Kelleys Island.

- C.W. 2006

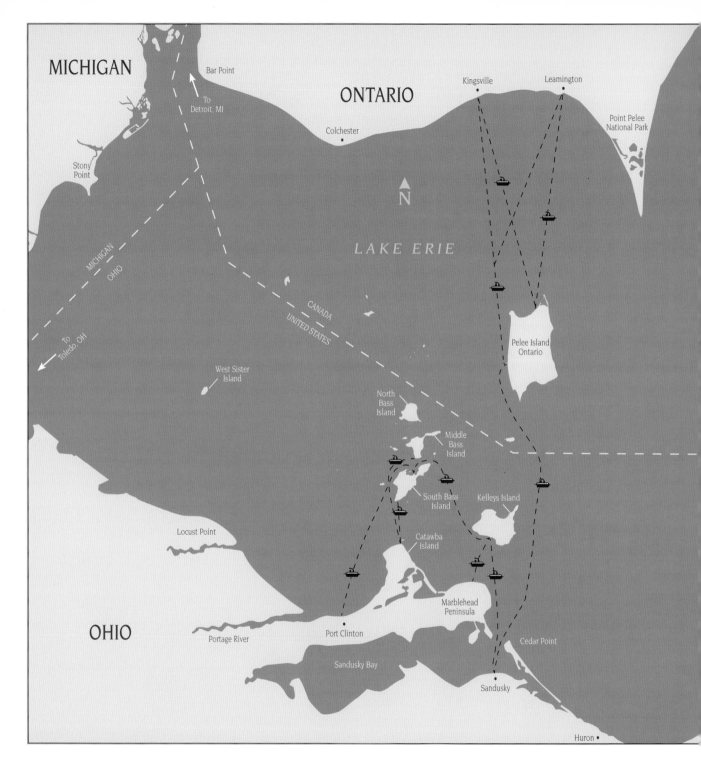

Table of Contents:

An Overview
of Ohio's Lake Erie Islands

Seen from the air, the shallow western basin of Lake Erie is spotted with a number of randomly shaped, tree-covered islands that seem to float on the water's surface. These islands, divided between Canada and the United States, are in fact projections of limestone and dolomite, carved by glacial activity 10,000 – 12,000 years ago, and since eroded by the effects of wind and water. Where present, the islands' dense groundcover consists of typical eastern woodland forest, overgrown with creeping grapevines and native red cedar trees. Wildlife flourishes on the Lake Erie islands, including a wide variety of migratory and other large birds, as well as deer, foxes, turtles, snakes, and a handful of protected plant and animal species found only on these remote outposts. One such animal is the Lake Erie water snake, a subspecies of the common water snake that has uniquely adapted to a life of fishing on the open lake.

Lake Erie, the fourth largest of the Great Lakes in terms of surface area, is actually the smallest when measured by water volume, due to a relatively shallow average depth of 62 feet. It is also the southernmost of all the Great Lakes, and is subject to a variety of extremes in temperature and weather, from Mediterranean summers to near-Arctic winters.

Bordered by Ohio, Michigan, Pennsylvania, New York and Ontario, Canada, Lake Erie has weathered more of the negative effects of urbanization and agriculture than perhaps any of the other Great Lakes. Despite

Long Point on Kelleys Island

this, and with the help of recent environmental efforts, Lake Erie continues to produce more fish for human consumption than all of the other Great Lakes combined.

The number of islands in western Lake Erie has been disputed over the years, as some "islands" are little more than exposed reefs, while others – such as Catawba Island and Johnson's Island – are now connected to the mainland. The main group of islands situated off the coast of Port Clinton and Sandusky, Ohio, are known collectively as the Bass Island Archipelago. When viewed on a map, the archipelago appears as a series of stepping-stones that reaches across the lake from the United States to Canada. Ownership of the 23 "true" islands has been established over the past 300 years; 14 are part of Ohio, while nine are found in Canadian waters. Kelleys, the largest of the American isles at about four square miles, is dwarfed by Canada's Pelee, the largest, at about 16.5 square miles.

Of the U.S. islands, today only Kelleys, South Bass and Middle Bass have regular ferry and air services from the mainland. North Bass and Rattlesnake islands can be reached by airplane or an occasional ferry; however, the others can only be reached by private boat. The most daring travelers reach the

Looking north over South Bass Island

islands across the ice via snowmobile, airboat, ATV or even car during the winter months.

Currently, only eight of the 14 Ohio islands in the archipelago are inhabited – several only seasonally – although a few of the deserted islands were previously occupied in historic times. Four of these eight islands provide year-round residence to a handful of hardy individuals, who have developed a unique culture and lifestyle much different than that on the mainland.

These islands have long and illustrious histories, beginning with early American Indian occupation, and continuing through historic naval battles and celebrated fishing and winery ventures. Today, many of the larger islands have evolved into popular summer home and vacation destinations, and are visited by thousands of people each year.

The islands themselves offer significant diversity to visitors: from the desolation of North Bass, to the hustle and bustle of Put-In-Bay, to the laid-back attitude on Middle Bass, or the rural atmosphere of Kelleys. It is still possible, however, with a boat or a bike and some time, to get away from the crowds and experience the islands as they once were – sunlight, solitude and the waves gently lapping at the shore...

Cedar Point as seen from Kelleys Island in winter

A stretch of Kelleys' south shore in the fall

Kelleys Island

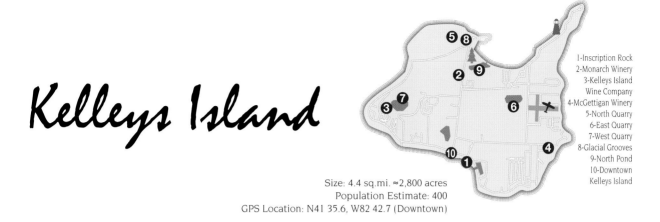

1-Inscription Rock
2-Monarch Winery
3-Kelleys Island
Wine Company
4-McGettigan Winery
5-North Quarry
6-East Quarry
7-West Quarry
8-Glacial Grooves
9-North Pond
10-Downtown
Kelleys Island

Size: 4.4 sq.mi. ≈2,800 acres
Population Estimate: 400
GPS Location: N41 35.6, W82 42.7 (Downtown)

At a little more than four square miles, Kelleys Island is the largest of all of the U.S. islands in Lake Erie. Located about three miles from the mainland, Kelleys bears evidence of early occupation by various American Indian groups. A number of burial mounds, walled enclosures, and stone petroglyphs attest to a significant pre-European presence in the area. One striking example is Inscription Rock, found on the south shore of the island, where the surface of a large limestone boulder has been decorated with carvings of various human and animal forms.

Formerly called Cunningham's Island after its first white settler, a little-known trader believed to have lived among the Indians on the island sometime between 1803 and 1808, Kelleys obtained its current name from the family of Datus and Irad Kelley of Rockport Township, located west of Cleveland, Ohio. Attracted by the high-quality limestone and cedar trees, the Kelley brothers bought 1,500 acres, or about half of the island, in 1833 for $1.50 an acre, and by 1836 owned most of the island. The Township of Kelleys Island was formally established in 1840.

Looking east over Kelleys Island, with the now-filled limestone quarries and a freighter in the foreground

Over the years, Kelleys Island has hosted a number of industries, including fishing, wine production and stone quarrying. From the late 1800s through the 1950s, the fishing industry thrived on Kelleys Island, as commercial boats plied the local waters for whitefish, pickerel (walleye), black bass, pike and muskellunge – to the extent that several species were subsequently fished out of Lake Erie.

Owing to gentle lake breezes and limestone soil, and because Lake Erie's waters afford the islands a slightly more temperate climate and longer growing season than the mainland, the islands have proven to be ideal for grape cultivation. The first vines were planted on Kelleys in the 1840s and 1850s, and soon after, the potential to make a living

Ruins of the Kelleys Island Wine Company, as seen from above and below

growing grapes for wine brought a number of immigrants to the island. By 1872, the permanent population grew into the thousands, primarily made up of Irish and German immigrant laborers.

Remnants of a grape harvester on the southeast side of Kelleys Island

At the peak of wine production, the southeastern part of the island was almost completely cleared and under grape cultivation. The furrows and descendants of the original grapevines can still be seen in the second-growth forests there. A lasting tribute to their former glory, the ruins of the Monarch Winery on Division Street and the Kelleys Island Wine Company near the west quarry (both on private property), are still standing today, as is the former McGettigan Winery near the east end of Woodford Road, which has been converted into a summer residence. At its peak in 1870, the Kelleys Island Wine Company had storage capacity in its cellars for 400,000 gallons of wine, and was one of the largest wine producers in the country. The success and profitability of grape cultivation was quickly replicated on many of the other Lake Erie islands – most significantly on the three Bass islands.

Ruins of the Monarch Winery on Division Street

Thanks to large quantities of exposed limestone located in close proximity to inexpensive water transportation, Kelleys has also hosted a number of quarrying operations over the years. The north quarry operated through the early 1900s, but by the Great Depression, operations focused on the better quality stone found in the east and west quarries. The limestone was quarried primarily for construction purposes, but was also burned in giant lime kilns on the island to produce powdered lime for cement and other applications. The east and west quarries closed just prior to World War II; however, the remains of many of the lime kilns and other quarry buildings can be seen at various locations around the island. In the 1990s, quarrying operations resumed at the west quarry on Bookerman Road, which was blasted out to a depth of over one hundred feet, but (as of this writing) ceased quarry operations at the end of 2008 – and has now re-filled itself to lake level with sparkling blue water. Both the north and east quarries are now owned by the Ohio Department of Natural Resources, and are managed as natural wildlife areas. Due to the technology of the era, neither quarry is particularly deep, and the water-filled east quarry now provides an excellent wetland habitat.

Sunset on the west quarry dock

Fall and winter at the east quarry

Today, Kelleys Island has a population estimated at around 400 residents, providing a warm, small-town atmosphere. There are some 700 houses on the island, most of which are seasonal summer cottages. The island also has a number of working farms, as well as bed and breakfasts, rental cottages, one hotel resort (as of this writing), and a state park campground with modern amenities and a sandy beach. Commercial establishments are limited to a handful of shops, restaurants and taverns.

Glacial grooves on Kelleys Island at sunset illustrate striations in the rock carved by glaciers

Near the sandy beach on the north shore, some of the world's finest examples of glacial grooves (striations in the stone made by glacial movement during the last ice age) can be viewed by visitors. The nearby North Pond State Preserve includes a lake-fed marsh that is home to a variety of plant and animal species.

Golf carts are street-legal on the islands, and summer visitors can enjoy leisurely island tours by golf cart or bike. Miles of hiking trails on state park property on the north shore and in the east quarry provide an opportunity for visitors to see the island in its pristine state, and to appreciate its natural beauty. Outstanding deer hunting and sport fishing on the island also provide a pastime for both visitors and locals year-round.

Ice fishing at Kelleys Island State Park

Perry's Memorial on South Bass Island

South Bass Island
(Put-in-Bay)

Size: 2.5 sq.mi.   ±600 acres
Population Estimate: 700
GPS Location: N41 39.2, W82 49.0 (Downtown)

1-Perry's Cave
2-Crystal Cave and
Heinemann Winery
3-Cannonball Monument,
De Rivera Park
4-Perry's Memorial
5-Fish Hatchery
6-Downtown Put-in-Bay
7-Scheeff East Point Nature Preserve
8-Lake Erie Islands Nature and Wildlife Center
9-Lake Erie Islands Historical Society Museum
10-De Rivera Woods

South Bass Island is located less than three miles from the mainland. Put-in-Bay is the formal name for both the township and village located on South Bass Island. The village encompasses only the "downtown" area near the harbor, while the township includes the rest of South Bass, plus Middle and North Bass islands, as well as Rattlesnake, Sugar, Ballast, Gibraltar, Green and Starve islands.

Originally known as Ross' Island, the origin of the name Put-in-Bay has been disputed over the years. Many historians note that early charts and logs of the island from the late 1700s refer to the harbor as "Hope's Cove" (named for a ship that wintered there in the ice) or as "Pudding Bay", possibly because of the soft, pudding-like consistency of the harbor's lake floor. Others believe that the name Put-in-Bay was coined by Commodore Oliver Hazard Perry, who stationed his ships in the harbor during the War of 1812.

Perry's Memorial towers over the Put-in-Bay Harbor on South Bass Island

The limestone strata that comprise much of the Bass islands have supported the development of a number of shallow, domed caves, especially on South Bass, where many of the caves were built upon and used as cellars or water wells for homes on the island. Several caves have been commercially developed for tourism over the years, although now only two – Crystal and Perry's – are open to the public. Evidence of early American Indian occupation of South Bass Island has also been documented, including the discovery of stone tools, burial mounds and even human skeletons purportedly cached in some of the island's caves.

The earliest white inhabitants of South Bass Island were French squatters who arrived in the early 1800s, but were driven off the island by caretakers of its owner, Alfred Pierpont Edwards of Connecticut. Edwards, a Revolutionary War veteran, had obtained the island – as well as Middle Bass, Sugar, Gibraltar, Ballast and Starve – for $26,087 in the 1807 Land Lottery of the Connecticut Western Reserve.

Celestine (strontium sulfate) crystals adorn the walls and ceiling of Crystal Cave on South Bass Island

In the summer and fall of 1811, Edwards had workers clear a few hundred acres of land on South Bass to plant wheat. This crop was destroyed by British soldiers in the fall of 1812, when they surprised the workers and drove them off the island; these islands were among the lands disputed in the War of 1812. Subsequent to this event, South Bass Island played a major role in the war by serving as the base of naval operations for U.S. Commodore Oliver Hazard Perry, whose ships engaged the British fleet near the coast of South Bass Island on September 10, 1813. The American victory in this pivotal naval battle – "We have met the enemy and they are ours" – secured Lake Erie for the Americans and allowed the United States to invade Canada, ultimately defeating the British the following month.

Both the British and American officers killed in the Battle of Lake Erie were ceremoniously laid to rest on South Bass in a common location near the harbor, which was marked by a lone willow tree until 1900. This spot in downtown's De Rivera Park is now marked by a monument of stacked cannonballs. In October 1912, construction was begun on a monument to mark the 100th anniversary of this battle, and in 1913

Put-in-Bay's lighthouse and tower on the southwest tip of the island

the officers' remains were moved to a crypt beneath the rotunda floor of the new monument. Perry's Victory and International Peace Memorial, completed and opened in June 1915, towers 350 feet above the lake level, rewarding visitors to its observation deck with a spectacular panoramic view of the islands.

Perry's victory and the end of the war with the British initiated the settlement and development of South Bass Island. This development picked up speed in 1854 when the Edwards family sold South Bass and the other five islands for $44,000 to Jose de Rivera St. Jurgo, a Spanish-born New York merchant. The harvesting of timber, commercial fishing, quarrying (for lime production), grape cultivation, and even ice production provided jobs and commercial growth to the island in its early years. When the cedar timber resources used for steamboat fuel were exhausted in the mid-1800s,

Grapevines on South Bass Island ready for harvest

De Rivera followed the lead of Kelleys Island and planted the first grapevines in 1858. The wine industry prospered, and soon South Bass had more than a dozen independent wineries, with over half the island under grape cultivation. Today only a few family vineyards and just one winery remain in operation. The Heinemann Winery, located at the intersection of Catawba Avenue and Thompson Road, is also home to Crystal Cave. The varieties of grapes typically grown on the islands include Niagara, Catawba, Concord, Ives and Delaware.

Commercial fishing also had its run as a major industry on South Bass. A fish hatchery built by the federal government in the late 1800s operated until the 1930s at Peach Point, just north of the harbor. The State of Ohio built its own hatchery nearby in 1925, although it is no longer in operation.

Having obtained electricity from the mainland in 1929, South Bass is now the most commercially developed of all the Lake Erie Islands. Used as a summer resort for more than 100 years, a multitude

Sticks, weeds and sometimes even Christmas trees are placed in the ice to mark safe routes between islands

of condominiums, hotels, marinas, bed and breakfasts, restaurants and water sports facilities are available for visitors, as well as a modern state park campground. The campground is built on the former site of the grandiose 625-room Hotel Victory which burned to the ground the night of August 14, 1919.

Put-in-Bay Harbor hosts countless boats during the summer months, and a vibrant nightlife adds thousands of visitors to the local population of around 700 residents, filling the 1,000 or so homes and cottages to capacity. South Bass is also a center for ice fishing, drawing anglers to the island between January and March, and ice shanties dot the area when temperatures permit the lake to freeze. Islanders have adapted to life in the deep freeze; many use snowmobiles, ATVs, flat-bottomed airboats, hovercrafts, or modified "ice cars" (with spiked tires and a cut-off top, should a quick exit become necessary) for inter-island transportation across the ice during the winter months.

A sailboat bobs in Put-in-Bay Harbor

The narrow arm of East Point on Middle Bass Island; Sugar Island is visible offshore in the distance

Middle Bass Island

Size: 1.3 sq.mi. ≈800 acres
Population Estimate: 50
GPS Location: N41 40.5, W82 48.4 (State Park Dock)

1-Kuehnle Marsh
2-Middle Bass
Schoolhouse
3-Middle Bass Club
4-Payer Mansion
5-Lonz Winery

Located less than a mile to the north of South Bass, Middle Bass Island is believed to have been the first of all the Lake Erie islands to be visited by Europeans. On August 6, 1679, Father Louis Hennepin, a Jesuit missionary under the leadership of the French explorer La Salle, reportedly sighted and came ashore with about 30 individuals from his boat, The Griffin, and celebrated Mass with a number of the American Indian residents. Father Hennepin christened the island "Île des Fleurs" (Island of Flowers) due to the prevalence of summer blooms that covered the landscape. Indian relics found on Middle Bass suggest that the island was used by early residents as a seasonal hunting ground, or perhaps as part of a stepping-stone route across the lake.

The unique shape of Middle Bass has resulted in the creation of a number of interesting natural areas. In historic times of high water or severe storms, Deist Road has flooded, causing the narrow eastern half of the island to become separated from the rest of the land mass, creating two distinct islands.

A snowy egret is at home in the Kuehnle Marsh on Middle Bass Island

The wetland area to the northwest of Deist Road is known as Kuehnle Marsh and is one of only three remaining lake-fed marsh areas on the U.S. islands; the others are on Kelleys and North Bass. The marsh is a beautiful natural area that is home to an abundance of plant and animal species. As on Kelleys, glacial grooves can also be found at various locations on Middle Bass Island.

Middle Bass Island had only one resident squatter prior to 1854, when a handful of German settlers came to the island to begin work in farming and the timber trade. By the late 1850s, the success of the wine and fishing industries on South Bass and Kelleys led to the dramatic growth of grape cultivation and commercial fishing ventures on Middle Bass.

While grape cultivation played a major role in the initial development and growth of the island, Middle Bass Island was also developed early on as a summer vacation resort. This was due, in part, to the island's relative seclusion one mile north of Put-in-Bay, affording visitors access to the amenities available there, while allowing Middle Bass to maintain a quieter existence as a secondary destination. The island hosted regular summer visits from such famous individuals as former U.S. Presidents Benjamin Harrison, Grover Cleveland, Rutherford B. Hayes and William Howard Taft – as well as numerous Ohio congressmen and governors.

The smartly painted schoolhouse on Middle Bass Island

In 1874, a group of Toledo businessmen bought and built a clubhouse on the western-most point of Middle Bass, eventually known as "The Middle Bass Club", in order to create an exclusive summer retreat for fishing, shooting and boating. Members bought parcels of land and built fantastic Victorian summer homes on the club's grounds, which eventually included a chapel, docks and boathouse, in addition to tennis courts, bowling alleys and a protective seawall. Summer weekends saw lively bands and other festivities at the clubhouse. Although the clubhouse and chapel have since been razed and several of the cottages destroyed by fire, the former club grounds still maintain a picturesque Martha's Vineyard-type atmosphere.

A collection of dormer windows on some of the historic Middle Bass Club homes

A Frank Lloyd Wright-style mansion built by Cleveland attorney Harry F. Payer in 1925 is located on private property, at the very tip of East Point. His 100-acre property once included an airport, golf course, stables and a game preserve. As a result, Middle Bass still maintains two landing strips on the island.

The Payer Mansion on East Point of Middle Bass

The former Lonz winery at the southern tip of the island dates back to one of Middle Bass' original settlers, German immigrant Andrew Wehrle, whose "Golden Eagle Wine Cellars" was established at the same location around 1870. A stonecutter by trade, Wehrle carved a 14-foot-deep wine cellar with a capacity of over a half million gallons out of the solid limestone, and added a huge dance pavilion above it. In 1926, Peter Lonz, an employee of Wehrle, began his own wine-making business and eventually took over Wehrle's operations, assisted by his son George. The Lonz family survived Prohibition by selling grape juice along with careful instructions on how to avoid fermentation – or induce it, depending on a customer's particular taste!

Following the repeal of Prohibition, George built the current Lonz building, a unique castle-like edifice. An observation tower was added during a re-build in 1941, after a fire destroyed a portion of the building. The Lonz Winery was managed by George Lonz until his death in 1968; however, the winery continued lively operations under corporate ownership until July 2000, when an

Lonz Winery on the southern tip of Middle Bass Island, now part of the state park

accident involving the collapse of a terrace forced closure. Just three months earlier, the State of Ohio had announced the purchase of 124 acres on Middle Bass, including the Lonz property and the many historic buildings located there. Since that time, the Middle Bass Island State Park has been established, which features boat docks, fishing, hiking and campground facilities.

Middle Bass Island is currently home to approximately 50 year-round residents, but the population swells during the summer months as seasonal residents arrive, filling the 350 houses that dot the island. The island can be reached by ferry from the mainland or South Bass Island, and by air from Sandusky or Port Clinton. Middle Bass has a limited number of retail enterprises, including a few stores and eating establishments.

An underwater reef extends offshore of the easternmost tip of Middle Bass Island

A fall day on North Bass Island, looking southwest near Fox's Marsh

North Bass Island

1-North Bass Chapel
2-Fox's Marsh

Size: 1.1 sq.mi. ≈700 acres
Population Estimate: Less than 20
GPS Location: N41 42.4, W82 48.9 (South Dock)

Located a mile north of Middle Bass and a mile from the Canadian border, North Bass Island shares much of its history with the other big islands. This includes the development of prosperous wine and fishing industries in the mid-1800s by a handful of American and Canadian pioneers. Although many of the original buildings have since been reclaimed by forest and vines, the island has changed very little since it was first settled, and remains the last large, undeveloped island in Lake Erie. North Bass was originally called Isle St. George, and the island still retains that name on its postmark. It is believed that the U.S. Postal Service adopted this name because they wanted to distinguish it from the other Bass Islands.

Looking southeast across North Bass Island with vineyards and Fox's Marsh in the foreground

With a full-time population of about two dozen people in the early 2000s, and no retail enterprises to speak of, the island has been primarily used for grape cultivation since the mid-1800s. North Bass Island has had a reputation as an outpost for only the most adventurous individuals, and in its early years produced a number of sea captains and fishermen.

Almost all of the people living on North Bass today are or were involved with growing grapes, although the total land under cultivation has decreased since its pre-Prohibition heyday. Except for a handful of private lots, ownership of the island has been passed through a number of corporate entities in recent years. Successive owners continued to cultivate a majority of the island for wine production and provided housing and supplies for the individuals employed there. However, in April 2004 the Ohio Department of Natural Resources acquired 87 percent of the island from its corporate owners for $17.4 million in order to protect it from development. While no ferry service is available to North Bass, future plans include the development of park facilities there.

The North Bass Chapel, formerly the Isle of St. George Congregational Church

North Bass has had electricity since 1958 and personal phone service since the 1990s. The island once claimed the smallest school district in the country, as well as the last one-room schoolhouse in Ohio which closed in 2005 when its last student graduated. Until recently, North Bass was served by one church, the Isle of St. George Congregational Church (now the North Bass Chapel), built around 1880.

One of many abandoned farmhouses overlooking a vineyard on North Bass Island

Roads on North Bass range from paved streets to dirt trails. North Bass is also home to Fox's Marsh, a lake-fed, 40-acre wetland area in the southwest portion of the island, where several endangered plant and animal species thrive. Visitors must arrive by plane or private boat, and need to arrange for their own land transportation.

Grape crates await pickup on the south dock of North Bass

Rattlesnake Island

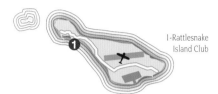

1-Rattlesnake
Island Club

Size: ≈64 acres
Population Estimate: Seasonal
GPS Location: N41 40.8, W82 51.2

Only one and a half miles to the northwest of South Bass is Rattlesnake Island, believed to have been given its name by American Indians due to its elongated, hump-back shape, and the two small rocky outcroppings off its western tip, known as the "rattles." Early maps actually refer to the whole group of islands as "Rattlesnake Islands"; perhaps early visitors had observed the Lake Erie water snake, which thrives on the rocky shorelines of most of the islands in the area.

Part of Put-in-Bay Township, Rattlesnake Island's 64 acres have been under private ownership since early settlement of the islands. In the 1800s, the island served as a residence and get-away for locals from Put-in-Bay and neighboring islands. In 1906, the island gained notoriety when a major steamship serving the islands ran aground on one of the "rattles." The island was eventually bought in 1929 by industrialist Hugh Bennett of Toledo, Ohio, who built two log cabins for his family there. Around that time, Prohibition laws were passed and Rattlesnake Island is reported to have had a major role in the import of illegal liquor from Canada.

The hump-back profile of Rattlesnake Island, as seen from Middle Bass

After World War II, Rattlesnake Island went through a series of creative, yet unsuccessful, business scenarios. First, the island was sold to a religious order of Catholic priests for use as a retreat. Shortly afterward, a group of doctors bought the island, intending to use it as a place for heart

Rattlesnake Island, with the two "rattles" in the foreground

patients to rest and recover. When this enterprise failed, a new owner attempted to operate a restaurant on the island called *The Golden Pheasant*.

Finally, in 1979, the island was acquired by a Cleveland businessman who developed the exclusive Rattlesnake Island Club, where members paid an annual fee for access to the elaborate clubhouse he had built there. Stories are still told of the club's private parties and the gun-toting security agents who would wave off boaters who came too near the shore. The club's amenities were further developed until 1998, when the island was put up for auction and purchased by a real estate investment group. This group has subsequently parceled off lots of land, as well as 65 club memberships, increasing the number of private homes on Rattlesnake to around 15.

Today, access to Rattlesnake Island is limited to residents and club members, who arrive via private boat or airplane as well as from occasional stops by the Middle Bass ferry. The island even established its own private local post airmail service in the 1960s, which recently resumed operations. Over the years, Rattlesnake Island has been home to a number of exotic animals, including llamas and bighorn sheep, and there is reported to still be a healthy pheasant population on the island.

Sugar Island

Size: ≈32 acres
Population Estimate: Seasonal
GPS Location: N41 41.5, W82 49.5

Part of Put-in-Bay Township, Sugar Island consists of 32 forested acres located about a quarter mile off the northwest coast of Middle Bass. Early maps sometimes showed the island to be attached to Middle Bass via the now submerged Sugar Island Reef – a local boating hazard.

Sugar Island in the fall, with a portion of its reef exposed

Originally used by local island residents for camping and fishing excursions, Sugar Island was part of the land purchased by Edwards in 1807, and has been handed down through a number of families over the years since.

Sugar Island currently has no public electricity or other amenities, but it includes several cottages and can be accessed only by private boat with the owners' permission. At times of very low water the island can be reached by foot, simply by wading across the reef from Middle Bass.

Mouse Island

Size: ≈7.5 acres
Population Estimate: Seasonal
GPS Location: N41 35.5, W82 50.0

Mouse Island, situated a mere thousand feet from the tip of Catawba Island (Catawba is now connected to the mainland), was first known as Hat Island, possibly due to its shape – having a narrow, brim-like reef extending from its western shore. Likely re-named for its small size (about seven acres), the island has been under private ownership since settlement and was once owned by the family of President Rutherford B. Hayes.

There was at one time a home on the island, rumored to have a tunnel beneath it connecting Mouse Island to the mainland at Catawba, and used either as part of the Underground Railroad, or possibly for liquor transport during the Prohibition era. The island may be visited only by private boat with permission of the owner.

Mouse Island as seen from the west

Ballast Island

Size: ≈12 acres
Population Estimate: Seasonal
GPS Location: N41 40.6, W82 47.1

Ballast Island as seen from the water

Ballast, a small island of less than a dozen acres, is situated one mile east of Middle Bass Island. This island reportedly obtained its name when Commodore Perry put in here prior to his battle with the British during the War of 1812, in order to take on ballast for his ships, using small boulders strewn on the island's shore.

Until the mid-1800s, the only resident of Ballast Island was a local hermit known simply as "Uncle Jimmy," who lived in an old weather-beaten cabin. About this time, the island was purchased by a group of Cleveland businessmen – including George Gardner, the mayor of Cleveland – who subsequently built homes, but apparently tolerated their local squatter. Some years later, during a rare trip to the mainland, Uncle Jimmy was killed in a fire aboard a steamship on its way to Sandusky. His neighbors on Ballast Island paid for a proper burial for Uncle Jimmy on Put-in-Bay.

The Western Canoe Association also called Ballast Island home from the late 1800s through the turn of the twentieth century, and Ballast was the scene of a number of canoe races, contests and other festivities at their clubhouse. The Gardner family's original log cabin, built in 1860 using island wood, is still owned and occupied seasonally by members of the Gardner family and is the oldest house on any of the islands.

Ballast Island today contains less than a dozen private residences, and most owners are related. Residents share the cost of a private electrical generator serving several of the houses on the island. Access is limited to residents by private boat only.

Ballast Island in fall

Gibraltar Island

Size: ≈5 acres
Population Estimate: Seasonal
GPS Location: N41 39.5, W82 49.2

Gibraltar Island, labeled as George's Island or St. George's Island on early maps, covers no more than five acres of land surrounded by rocky cliffs, located almost in the center of Put-in-Bay Harbor between South and Middle Bass islands. The island originally gained its prominence as the location where Commodore Perry's lookout watched for the British fleet in 1812, as it includes the highest elevation on any of the islands.

Gibraltar was part of the original 1807 land purchase of Alfred P. Edwards, and like South Bass, was later owned by Jose de Riviera St. Jurgo. In 1864 the island was purchased for $3,000 by Sandusky Civil War financier Jay Cooke, who built a magnificent stone "castle" on the highest point of the island. Cooke was a generous donor and member of the island community, regularly opening his island and gardens to the public for picnics.

Gibraltar Island in Put-in-Bay Harbor

In 1925, Gibraltar was sold to Julius Stone of Columbus, Ohio, who presented Gibraltar to The Ohio State University. The island is now part of Ohio State's campus, and includes resident housing and classroom facilities for a variety of biological studies. Gibraltar can only be reached by private boat, and is open to the public one day each year.

Cooke Castle in fall

A fall view through the naturally-formed archway known as the "Needle's Eye" on the northeast shore of Gibraltar Island, just below "Perry's Lookout", looking at Put-in-Bay Harbor's east shore

West Sister Island

Size: ≈77 acres
Population Estimate: 0
GPS Location: N41 44.2, W83 06.6

West Sister Island, the farthest-flung island in the archipelago, is located 14 miles to the northwest of North Bass Island and is currently a National Wildlife Refuge under the control of the U.S. Fish and Wildlife Service. In historic times, this unlikely location was home to the family of the first doctor serving Put-in-Bay and the other Lake Erie islands. During the War of 1812, Perry's victory over the British occurred just offshore of West Sister Island.

Containing what is believed to be the largest heron and egret rookery in the Great Lakes, the island has the distinction of being designated in 1975 as the only Wilderness Area in the state of Ohio, and it can only be visited with government permission for research purposes. Five acres on the western side of the island are owned by the Coast Guard to maintain the lighthouse there. Originally constructed around 1848 and renovated in 1868, the lighthouse was managed by an in-residence keeper until it was automated in 1937.

Although established as a Wildlife Refuge by President Franklin D. Roosevelt, West Sister was used for aircraft artillery practice by the U.S. War Department from 1945 to 1951, which destroyed the lighthouse keeper's quarters. Today, only the lighthouse remains, marking the western edge of the South Passage through the Lake Erie islands.

The West Sister Island lighthouse overlooks a frozen Lake Erie (Photo courtesy John Marvin, www.greatlakeslighthouses.com)

Green Island

Size: ≈20 acres
Population Estimate: 0
GPS Location: N41 38.7, W82 52.1

Green Island, situated one mile west of South Bass Island, is currently owned by the federal government under the jurisdiction of the U.S. Fish and Wildlife Service. The island is managed by the Ohio Department of Natural Resources as a wildlife refuge. The U.S. government has operated a lighthouse on Green Island since 1855.

Green Island, with the lighthouse tower in the foreground

Slightly smaller than Sugar Island, Green was also part of Alfred P. Edwards' original 1807 land purchase. For a number of years, the U.S. government had approached Edwards expressing interest in acquiring some island property from him to build a lighthouse to mark the islands for transport ships traveling Lake Erie between Detroit, Cleveland and Buffalo. As the story goes, they were pressing him for parts of South Bass or Rattlesnake Island; however, Edwards refused, not wanting to parcel off any piece of land. He finally relented and sold them all of Green Island in 1851.

After the government completed its first lighthouse on Green Island in 1855, the only residents were the lighthouse keepers and their families. The property included a barn, pasture and a few small buildings. This lighthouse burned famously on New Year's Eve of 1863, and a new one built the following year. The new beacon remained in service until 1939, when the Coast Guard erected an automatic light on a steel tower. Since that time, the island has been left to grow wild, save for an occasional visit by government employees or researchers. The old lighthouse structure was burned by vandals in the 1950s, and now only its stone skeleton remains, along with the ruins of the other buildings, hidden among the trees and overgrowth.

Of special note, Green Island has a number of interesting geographical features, including glacial grooves, small caves and numerous veins of celestine (strontium sulfate) crystals, a mineral also found on Put-in-Bay, but in few other places of the world. For many years the island was officially known as Strontian Island (and Moss Island before that), as it was the principal source of strontium mineral specimens among collectors.

Green Island is a protected area for wildlife, and home to an abundance of birds, snakes and other animals. Government permission is required to visit the island, and because there is no dockage, the use of a kayak, canoe or rowboat is necessary to come ashore.

The 1864 lighthouse on Green Island, as it stands today

Starve Island

Size: ≈1 acre
Population Estimate: 0
GPS Location: N41 37.6, W82 49.3

Located a half mile off the southeast shore of South Bass Island, Starve Island consists of nothing more than a small limestone reef with a few trees and bushes. The island is merely the exposed portion of the Starve Island Reef, a local danger for boaters in the area. Approach is possible only by kayak, canoe or rowboat on the very calmest of days.

Starve Island as seen from above

Starve Island is home to a number of shore birds and water snakes, and the noise of the birds – and sometimes their odor – can be noticed from miles away. Starve Island is reported to have gotten its name from the story of a stranded sailor, whose skeleton was found on the island at some unknown point in history. The details of this story have been lost, as has an explanation of how someone could have starved to death so close to a well-populated island. Ironically, Starve Island was alternately labeled on early maps as "Dinner Island" and also as "Glacial Island".

Buckeye Island

Size: <1 acre
Population Estimate: 0
GPS Location: N41 39.9, W83 47.5

Buckeye Island, a small exposed reef covered with bushes and trees (including native buckeye trees), is located off the northeastern tip of South Bass Island.

The island is often accessible by foot across a shallow reef, especially in the fall and during times of low water. Over the years, this island has

Buckeye Island, offshore to the northeast of Put-in-Bay

been shown on maps to be a part of South Bass Island and, at times, a separate island. Historic photographs show that around the late 1800s or early 1900s there was, in fact, a residence on Buckeye Island, although nothing remains of it today.

Lost Ballast Island

Size: <1 acre
Population Estimate: 0
GPS Location: N41 40.5, W82 47.1

Lost Ballast Island, a small reef covered by bushes, lies just offshore of Ballast Island. Lost Ballast is connected to Ballast Island by an underwater reef, and it is never known to have been occupied. Further, Lost Ballast is not recognized on most maps due to its small size. As with the other reef islands, Lost Ballast is occupied only by birds and snakes.

Lost Ballast Island and some of its feathered residents

Gull Island

Size: 0 acres
Population: 0
GPS Location: N41 39.5, W82 42.2

Currently, Gull Island exists only as a shallow underwater shoal almost three miles north of Kelleys Island. Many older maps still show this navigational hazard as an island (labeled as "Ship Island"), although it has not been seen above the surface of the lake since the late 1800s, except possibly during severe seiches (pronounced "sayshes").

A seiche is an interesting Lake Erie phenomenon – commonly seen in smaller bodies of water – which occurs when a strong, prolonged wind (usually from the west and in the fall), blows a large volume of the water in the lake eastward toward Buffalo. This results in a drop in the lake level of the shallow Western Basin, and a corresponding increase on the eastern side of the lake – often in the course of a mere day. Seiches typically expose a great deal of the lake floor, with the largest one on record for Lake Erie being a 16-foot drop in water level!

In the 1700s – 1800s, it was said that during calm weather there was just room enough for a couple to spread out a picnic blanket for a lunch. At some future date, Gull Island may again make an appearance, should lake levels drop sufficiently.

Gull Island today

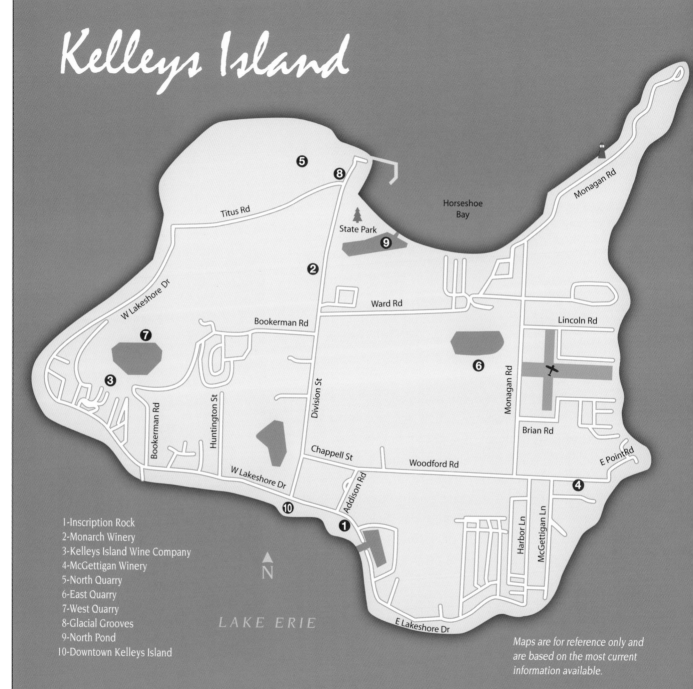

Kelleys Island

LAKE ERIE

1-Inscription Rock
2-Monarch Winery
3-Kelleys Island Wine Company
4-McGettigan Winery
5-North Quarry
6-East Quarry
7-West Quarry
8-Glacial Grooves
9-North Pond
10-Downtown Kelleys Island

Maps are for reference only and are based on the most current information available.

South Bass Island
(Put-in-Bay)

Buckeye Island

Columbus Ave

Chapman

Gibralter Island

Put-in-Bay Harbor

⑤ Fish Hatchery

W Shore Blvd

Mitchell Rd

Dahlgren Ave

Trenton Ave

Catawba Ave

Catawba Ave

Concord

③ ⑥ Delaware Ave

Bayview Ave ④

⑨

Langram Rd

① Catawba Ave

② ⑩ Tompson Rd

Niagara

State Park

Put-in-Bay Rd

Meechen Rd

⑧

Put-in-Bay Rd

Langram Rd

Airline Dr

N

LAKE ERIE

Starve Island

1-Perry's Cave
2-Crystal Cave and Heinemann Winery
3-Cannonball Monument, De Rivera Park
4-Perry's Memorial
5-Fish Hatchery
6-Downtown Put-in-Bay
7-Scheeff East Point Nature Preserve
8-Lake Erie Islands Nature and Wildlife Center
9-Lake Erie Islands Historical Society Museum
10-De Rivera Woods

Middle Bass Island

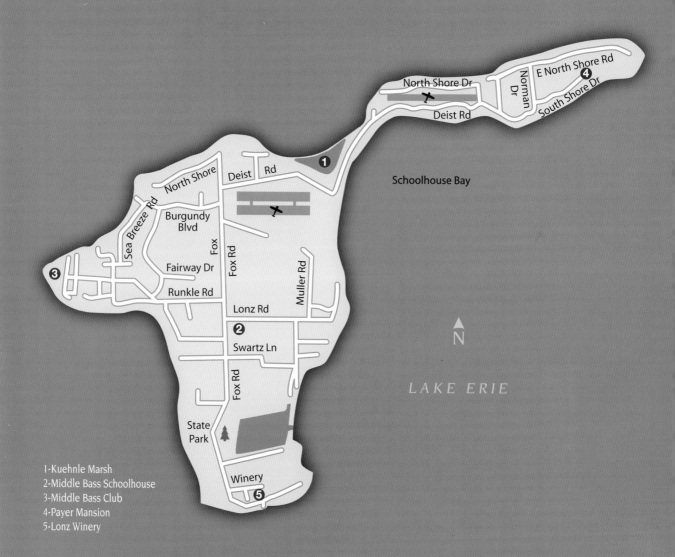

North Shore Dr

Deist Rd

Norman Dr

E North Shore Rd

South Shore Dr

❹

Schoolhouse Bay

Deist Rd

❶

North Shore

Sea Breeze Rd

Burgundy Blvd

Fox

Fox Rd

Muller Rd

Fairway Dr

❸

Runkle Rd

Lonz Rd

❷

Swartz Ln

N

LAKE ERIE

Fox Rd

State Park

Winery

❺

1-Kuehnle Marsh
2-Middle Bass Schoolhouse
3-Middle Bass Club
4-Payer Mansion
5-Lonz Winery

North Bass Island

Wires Rd

Peeple Rd

Sharon Dr

Tuhan Rd

Tuhan Rd

❶

Manila Bay

❷

Peeple Rd

Kenny Rd

Meiers Rd

▲
N

LAKE ERIE

1-North Bass Chapel
2-Fox's Marsh

REFERENCES

Barr, Henry. *Middle Bass Ohio – 1877 to 1977, Middle Bass Centennial Booklet, 1977.* Reprinted by Lake Erie Islands Historical Society, Put-in-Bay, Ohio, 2003

Brown, David. 1994. "Inside Put-in-Bay". February 2006. http://www.boats.com/content/default_detail.jsp?contentid=1793.

www.census.gov. Kelleys Island Village, Put-in-Bay Township, and Put-in-Bay Village. February 2006. http://factfinder.census.gov/home/saff/main.html.

DeLuca, Helen R. *The Lake Erie Islands and How They Got Their Names.* Pamphlet produced for the Historic Lyme Church, Ohio, 1974.

Dodge, Robert J. *Isolated Splendor: Put-in-Bay and South Bass Island.* Hicksville, New York: Exposition Press, 1975.

Downhower, Jerry F. *The Biogeography of the Island Region of Western Lake Erie.* Columbus, Ohio: Ohio State University Press, 1988.

Eiler, Lyntha and Terry. "Yesterday Lingers on Lake Erie's Bass Islands", *National Geographic*, Vol. 154, No. 1. (July 1978), pg. 86-101.

www.epa.gov. 2003. "The Great Lakes: An Environmental Atlas and Resource Book". February 2006. http://www.epa.gov/glnpo/atlas/ index.html.

www.firelandswinery.com. 2004. "Lonz Winery History". February 2006. http://www.firelandswinery.com/lonz/history.html.

www.fws.gov. West Sister Island National Wildlife Refuge. February 2006. http://www.fws.gov/midwest/ottawa/wsister.html.

Garmin Software. Mapsource: US Topo, Eastern United States V4.09. 1999-2002.

Genheimer, Robert A. *Cultures Before Contact: The Late Prehistory of Ohio and Surrounding Regions.* Columbus, Ohio: Ohio Archaeological Council, 2000.

Gora, Michael. 2004. "How Many Islands Are There in Lake Erie?", February 2006. http://www.middlebass2.org/IslandsInLakeErie.PDF.

Gora, Michael. Personal Interviews and Correspondence, 2005-2006.

Gora, Michael. Editor. *Sketches and Stories of the Lake Erie Islands*, by Lydia J. Ryall. Originally published by The American Publishers Company, 1913. Reprinted with supplementary materials by Lake Erie Islands Historical Society, Put-in-Bay, Ohio. Printed in Victoria, British Columbia: Trafford Publishing, 2004.

Gora, Michael. *Early Adventures at Put-on-Bay, Middle Bass, and Johnson's Island*, Raleigh, NC: Lulu.com, 2008.

www.great-lakes.net. 2006. Great Lakes Facts and Figures. February 2006. http://www.great-lakes.net/lakes/ref/lakefact.html.

Huntley, Melinda, and Weber, Art. "*Explore the Lake Erie Islands – A Guide to Nature and History along the lake Erie Costal Ohio Trail*". Pamphlet published by The Lake Erie Costal Trail National Scenic Byway, The Ohio Chapter of The Nature Conservancy, and Ohio Sea Grant, 2009

Illustrated Port Clinton and Environs: Embracing Port Clinton, Catawba Island, and Put-in-Bay. Port Clinton, Ohio: B.B. Krammes, 1898. Reprinted by Lake Erie Islands Historical Society, Put-in-Bay, Ohio, 2003.

www.kelleysislandchamber.com. 2005. Island Information and Island History. February 2006. http://www.kelleysislandchamber.com/default1.htm.

Kelleys Island Treasures. Pamphlet of the Kelleys Island Audubon Club, Kelleys Island, Ohio, undated (est. 2000 – 2004).

Kissel, Jeff. *Put-In-Bay: The Construction of Perry's Monument.* Chicago, Illinois: Arcadia Publishing, 2001.

www.lighthousefriends.com. 2001-2005. West Sister Island and Green Island. February 2006. http://www.lighthousefriends.com/pull-lights.asp.

Ligibel, Ted and Wright, Richard. *Island Heritage: A Guided Tour to Lake Erie's Bass Islands.* Columbus, Ohio: Ohio State University Press, 1987.

Linhardt, Becky. *Kelleys Island: An Island for All Seasons.* Kelleys Island, Ohio: Kelleys Cove, 1995.

www.middlebass.org. 2001-2005. News, Events, General Info., Photos, and History. February 2006. http://www.middlebass.org/.

www.nps.gov. "Lake Erie Islands" February 2006. http://www.nps.gov/pevi/HTML/islands.html.

Neale, Rick. "North Bass Island – Changes Loom for Tiny, Isolated Community", *Port Clinton News Herald*, October 25, 2003.

Newell, Amy L. *The Caves of Put-in-Bay.* New Washington, Ohio: Herald Printing, 1995.

Nichols, G.G. *Nichols' Handy Guide Book to Put-in-Bay, Middle Bass and Kelley's Island.* Sandusky, OH: I.F. Mack & Bro., 1888. Reprinted by Lake Erie Islands Historical Society, Put-in-Bay, Ohio, 2003.

www.odnr.com. Middle Bass Island State Park. February 2006. http://www.odnr.com/parks/parks/middlebass.htm.

ww.osu.edu. Gibraltar Island and South Bass Island. February 2006. http://www.osu.edu/cookecastle/island01c.html.

"Rattlesnake Island to be Auctioned" and **"Rattlesnake Has Interesting History".** *The Put-in-Bay Gazette*, Section B, September 1998, pg. 21-22.

Reinert, Linda. Personal Communications, 2005-2006.

State of Ohio, Office of the Governor. May 17, 2000. Press Release: *Governer Announces Plan to Acquire 123-Acre Lakefront Site on Middle Bass Island as Major Addition to Ohio State Parks.* http://www.ohiodnr.com/news/may00/MiddleBassIsland.htm.

State of Ohio, Office of the Governor. December 11, 2003. Press Release: *Taft Announces Plan to Preserve North Bass Island.* http://www.dnr.state.oh.us/news/dec03/1211northbass.htm.

www.tntn.essortment.com. 2002. "Lake Erie Islands". February 2006. http://www.tntn.essortment.com/lakeserieislan_rjob.htm.

Wells, John. *The History and Local Post of Rattlesnake Island, Lake Erie.* Knebworth, England: Able Publishing, 2003.

Wittemann, Adolph. *Lake Erie Islands: Put-in-Bay, Gibraltar, Middle Bass, Kelley's, etc.* New York, 1886. Reprinted by Lake Erie Islands Historical Society, Put-in-Bay, Ohio, 2003.

Acknowledgements

Thanks to my wife, Nicole, as well as my children Jake, Kade, and Avery for their love and support of this effort. It has been a pleasure to watch them grow up with the same love for this special place that I have. Also, thanks to my pilot, Tony Dracka, and my other travel companions for their bravery on the many research expeditions needed to make this book possible. Much appreciation to my editors – Mike Gora, Curt Harler and Bruce Waffen, for their patience, insight, criticism and support. A special thanks to Vince Adamo of The Adamo Group for his creative eye and design expertise in laying out this book. Finally, thanks to John Marvin of Marvin Aerial Photography for letting me borrow the one picture I was too scared to take myself.

C. W. 2006